THE DIVINE DRAMA OF JOB
SHORT COURSE SERIES - LARGE PRINT EDITION

CHARLES F. AKED, D.D.

ALICIA EDITIONS

CONTENTS

General Preface   5

1. THE INSURRECTION OF DOUBT   9
   1. The Plot.   10
   2. Author and Origin.   13
   3. The Great Polemic.   17

2. THE RESTORATION OF FAITH   21
   1. God in the Soul of Man.   21
   2. The God Above All.   25
   3. The Real Rewards or Righteousness.   28
   4. Ultima Veritas.   29

3. SATAN IN LITERATURE AND IN LIFE   31
   Satan in the Prologue.   32
   Insinuations against Job.   34
   Blasphemies against the Race.   35
   Satan in World-Literature.   37

4. ELIPHAZ THE SEER   41
   The First Speech of Eliphaz.   42
   The Failure of the Speech.   44
   The Second Speech of Eliphaz.   46
   The Third Speech of Eliphaz.   48
   The Salvation or Eliphaz.   50

5. BILDAD THE SAGE   52
   Bildad's Second Speech.   53
   The Third Speech or Bildad.   55
   Defences of Clay.   56
   The Appeal to Antiquity.   57

6. ZOPHAR THE ORDINARY SOUL   61
   Zophar's First Speech.   62
   Zophar's Second Speech.   65
   Gospel-hardened.   67
   The Triple Blunder.   69

7. THE INTERVENTION OF ELIHU   75
   The Contribution of Elihu.   76
   The Grace of Chastisement.   79
   The Justice of God.   81
   The Impossibility of Injustice.   83
   Love as Justice.   85

8. THE SPEECHES OF JEHOVAH   88
   The "Answer" of Jehovah.   90
   The Value of Christian Evidences.   93
   The Soul Subdued by Vastness.   96
   The Epilogue.   99

APPENDIX   102
Some Additional Reading   102

GENERAL PREFACE

The title of the present series is a sufficient indication of its purpose. Few preachers, or congregations, will face the long courses of expository lectures which characterised the preaching of the past, but there is a growing conviction on the part of some that an occasional short course, of six or eight connected studies on one definite theme, is a necessity of their mental and ministerial life. It is at this point the projected series would strike in. It would suggest to those who are mapping out a scheme of work for the future a variety of subjects which might possibly be utilised in this way.

The appeal, however, will not be restricted to ministers or preachers. The various volumes will meet the needs of laymen and Sabbath-school teachers who are interested in a scholarly but also practical exposition of Bible history and doctrine. In the hands of office-bearers and mission-workers the "Short Course Series" may easily become one of the most convenient and valuable of Bible helps.

It need scarcely be added that while an effort has been made to secure, as far as possible, a general uniformity in the scope and character of the series, the final responsibility for the special interpretations and opinions introduced into the separate volumes, rests entirely with the individual contributors.

A detailed list of the authors and their subjects will be found at the close of each volume.

"I loathe my life ; I would not live alway:
  Let me alone ; for my days are vanity."

—JOB VII. 16.

"Must it not be a deep spiritual instinct that drives trouble into solitude? . . . Away from the herd flies the wounded deer; away from the flock staggers the sickly sheep—to the solitary covert to die. The man too thinks it is to die; but it is in truth so to return to life. 'Leave me to my misery,' cries the man, and lo, his misery is the wind of the waving garments of him that walks in the garden in the cool of the day! All misery is *God unknown*."

— GEO. MACDONAL D.

CHAPTER I
THE INSURRECTION OF DOUBT

"Towering up alone, far away above all the poetry of the world"—so runs the famous criticism of the Book of Job pronounced by one of the most noted men of letters of the nineteenth century.[1] Did Carlyle influence Froude in this opinion as in some others? At least Froude may have been driven to study Job afresh when Carlyle's Heroes fell into his hands, some thirteen years before he wrote his luminous exposition. Carlyle would have it that Job, "apart from all theories about it," is "one of the grandest things ever written with pen." "A noble book," he insists; "all men's book... grand in its sincerity, in its simplicity, in its epic melody, and repose of reconcilement." And he multiplies words of admiration, indeed, of awe: "Sublime sorrow, sublime reconciliation; oldest choral melody as of the heart of mankind;—so soft and great; as the summer midnight, as the world with its seas and stars. There is nothing written, I think, in the Bible or out of it, of equal literary merit.[2]"

1. THE PLOT.

Job is a man, in the far-off patriarchal days, rich in herds and flocks; rich, too, in sons and daughters; rich in the esteem of all his world, honoured, powerful, and great. After calamity falls upon him he looks back with blended pride and sadness to the time of his prosperity:

> "When I went forth to the gate unto the city.
> When I prepared my teat in the street,
> The young men saw me and hid themselves,
> And the aged rose up and stood:
> The princes refrained from talking,
> And laid their hand on their mouth;
> The voice of the nobles was hushed,
> And their tongue cleaved to the roof of their mouth.
> For when the ear heard me, then it blessed me;
> And when the eye saw me, it gave witness unto me:
> Because I delivered the poor that cried,
> The fatherless also, that had none to help him.

> The blessing of him that was ready to perish came upon me;
> And I caused the widow's heart to sing for joy."
>
> —JOB XXIX. 7-13.

Unmerciful disaster brings him very low. A robber band sweeps down upon his oxen and his asses and carries them away, and his men-servants they put to the sword. Other bandits carry off his camels and kill the young men in charge of them. A fire destroys his sheep. And then a "great wind from the wilderness smote the four corners of the house" in which his children held high festival, so that seven tall sons and three fair daughters die together. Job is attacked by a loathsome disease. Bereaved, afflicted, lonely, "steeped in poverty to the very lips," like many of the distressed amongst the children of men before his day and since, he "wished that he had never been born."

Friends come to condole with him. They are three in number, Eliphaz, Bildad, and Zophar, men of strangely diverse temperament and habit of mind. They come to him in entire friendliness. They approach him with respect, even with reverence, for they have not to be told that sorrow like this sorrow is a sacred thing. Seven days and seven nights they sit upon the ground near to him, their garments rent, with ashes on their heads. And "none spake a word unto him; for they saw that his grief was very great." When, however, Job begins to give sorrow words, his friends are shocked, and, very mildly at first, with consideration and deference and tenderness, they venture to remonstrate with him and entreat him to restrain the utterances of grief which seem to them profane. And when Job, unrelieved by their sympathy and unconsoled by their preaching, persists in his outcry against the evil fate which has overwhelmed him, they lose patience and roundly reproach him. They do more. They tell him, in effect, that in some way he has brought these misfortunes on himself. Though they cannot lay their hands upon the secret sin which has called down upon him the judgment of an offended God, yet they are very sure that such secret sin there is. His protestations of innocence are in their eyes added proof of guilt. God has ordained that light shall shine upon the ways of the righteous man while the lamp of the sinner shall be put out. Had not Job so deeply sinned he would not now so deeply suffer. And since his sufferings are visible unto all men it cannot but be that heaven has visited upon him the recompense of his guilt. His denials add hypocrisy to iniquity and crown disobedience with insolent defiance of the Most High!

These charges, false and foolish as they are, and false as Job knows them to be, increase his misery. To the gloom in which he sits they add the horror of a great darkness which can be felt. And still the accusations are piled up against him. They grow more pointed, more definite, as the controversy proceeds. They deepen in intensity. They increase in violence. And Job writhes beneath them. They are false, and though every living human being pronounce them true he knows them false. Though earth go reeling back to chaos he will yet deny and denounce and damn the slanders which affront his soul.

Before the end Jehovah intervenes. Although Job did not know it, Jehovah, in the days of the great man's prosperity, had affirmed the righteousness of His servant's life. He had said that there was none like him on the earth. He had described Job as an upright and a perfect man, one who feared God and turned from evil. Now He sternly rebukes the friends who so misrepresent Him to the suffering man. His wrath is kindled against them because they have not spoken of Him "the thing that is right." And Jehovah "turned the captivity of Job" and gave him twice as much as he had before. Oxen and sheep and camels were multiplied to him; sons and daughters were born to him: in the land were found no women so fair as the daughters of Job: and his days were long in the land.

2. AUTHOR AND ORIGIN.

Is this story fact or fiction, history or parable? Did such a man as Job ever live, and did he experience these vicissitudes of fortune? Did his entire family of ten children die in one day, and then was that exact number of children born to him again in after years? Were seven thousand sheep destroyed and fourteen thousand restored to him? Three thousand camels destroyed and six thousand restored? And so with the asses and the oxen: did it really happen that precisely double the number lost were given to him again? And did Jehovah really deliver those long speeches, and if so, how did He deliver them? And who reported them? And how?

These questions answer themselves, and they go far to indicate the nature of the Book of Job. We are not here concerned with fact, not even with fact decked out in oriental hyperbole. *Job* is a work of imagination, a poem, a dramatic poem; and it is not any more fact than *Paradise Lost, Macbeth,* or *Faust.* It is poetry; it is philosophy; most of all, it is religion.

We need not inquire too particularly concerning the location of the land of Uz. It is a land of spirit. Neither do we need to establish the lineage of Job himself. Some suffering servant of Jehovah in some unknown age may have suggested to the unknown author the "plot" of his sublime drama, and some unwisely learned, affectionately cruel friends of the sufferer may have served the poet as models for his artistic creations, Eliphaz, Bildad, and Zophar. In this sense *Job* may be said to be "founded on fact." But such speculations are not free from a taint of pedantry, and in any case they do not carry us far. This is in truth "all men's book," and there is always in the land of Uz a man whose name is Job.

It is very wonderful to think that this book is anonymous. We, with our passion for publicity, and with our rigid views of the sacred rights of property in the children of our brain, can with difficulty think ourselves back to the mind of a day when a man of genius, one of the first-born of the sons of God, could give to the world a work greater than *Hamlet*, greater than the *Inferno*, greater than the *Critias*, and "scorn to blot it with a name." And our wonder deepens as we perceive that all the scholarship of all the A world has failed to find one shred of internal evidence which goes to establish the place of its origin or the century of its birth. From the time of Moses to the period of the Exile every century has been named by tradition or by criticism as the date of Job. A critic of international reputation[3] does indeed declare that "beneath the patriarchal disguise" may be discerned "the features of the author's own time," and that a late period in the history of Israel; that he "betrays familiarity with the law"; that he is "a true Israelite" and "betrays himself to be so at every turn." The ordinary reader of *Job* is a little chagrined by the reflection that he cannot discover for himself the ground of such dogmatic assurance. And he takes comfort from the mild protest of another scholar, held in equal honour by two continents,[4] "that other critics would demur to such decided phraseology," and that "it is certain that the book has to be searched very carefully before any traces of the law can be found in it, and these are not of a very pronounced kind." On the other hand, the references to life outside Israel, the amazing information which the writer possessed about the wonder-worlds in the lands beyond, and about their traditions, their myths, their cosmogony, startle and bewilder the reader at every turn and upset every theory as soon as it is advanced. "The life, the manners, the customs are of all varieties and places—Egypt, with its river and its pyramids, is there; the description of mining points to Phoenicia; the settled life in cities, the nomad Arabs, the wandering caravans, the heat of the tropics, and the ice of the north, all are foreign to Canaan, speaking of foreign things and foreign people. . . We look to find the three friends vindicate themselves, as they so well might have done, by appeals to the fertile annals of Israel, to the Flood, to the cities of the plain, to the plagues of Egypt, or the thunders of Sinai. But of all this there is not a word; they are passed by as if they had no existence; and instead of them, when witnesses are required for the power of God, we have strange un-Hebrew stories of the eastern astronomic mythology, the old war of the giants, the imprisoned Orion, the wounded dragon, the sweet influences of the seven stars, and the glittering fragments of the sea-snake Rahab trailing across the northern sky."[5] And it is not strange that in the presence of these phenomena the reader exclaims that the "scenes, the names, and the incidents, are all contrived as if to baffle curiosity." The author of *Job* remains the Great Unknown of literature.

3. THE GREAT POLEMIC.

The theme of the Book of Job is the world-old problem of pain and mystery of evil, against which the thinkers of the race have beaten their brains for twice two thousand years. One after another, Bible writers have looked the difficulty boldly in the face —and passed on! The author of the thirty-seventh Psalm—some sweet-natured, kind old man— concluded that it was best not to fret over such perplexing things, for worry tends only to wickedness.[6] He was satisfied that the wicked might grow to great power and spread himself like a green tree in his native soil, but that soon one would look for him in vain. While as to the righteous, he declared—

> "I hare been young, and now am old,
> Yet hare I not seen the righteous forsaken,
> Nor his seed begging bread."

But the author of Job could have told him that if he had not seen the righteous forsaken others had, and had likewise seen the seed of the righteous begging bread! The writer of the seventy-third Psalm, one of the most characteristic and significant in the whole Psalter, frankly confessed that the matter was to him unthinkable,[7] until he, too, found refuge from the burden of it in the forced belief which orthodoxy prescribed that the end of the sinner would be violence and death.

Upon such elementary "solutions" of his problem the author of *Job* flings scorn. There is one answer to them, and only one; but that is final and irrefutable; they are not true! They are not true to the facts of life. And men would not go on saying these things if others had not said them before. They are taught to say them. And generation by generation the tongues of men repeat them, though their minds, if they would but use their minds, yield no consent to them. These "solutions" are cheap and easy. They have become recognised formulas, and men have "swallowed formulas." The word was not then known, but the spirit of it breathes in Job's passionate speeches; these sayings are mere "cant"—cant, be it understood, properly defined as "unrealised phraseology," words which are supposed to cover a situation though their precise import has not once been seriously considered by the persons who repeat them so glibly. It is simply not true that virtue will find its sure reward in a life exempt from sickness, pain, and sorrow. It is not true that a violation of the laws of right will be followed by immediate, overwhelming calamity. Habits which constitute "righteousness" do on the whole and in the long run make for prosperity, while unrighteousness blinds and paralyses and destroys so that on the whole and in the long run the wages of sin is death. But in *Job* the accumulated miseries which befall the hero are not the consequence of his transgression. And on any broad view of the many-coloured life of man upon this earth some other explanation of the presence and pressure of sorrow must be found. On this tremendous subject the author of Job sets himself to broaden the thought of the world.

Then what is his "solution?" What explanation does he offer? None, absolutely none. In the wonderful Book of Job this is perhaps the most wonderful thing. The opening chapter supplies a prologue to the drama. There we are introduced into the Court of Heaven. We see that the Satan is given permission by Jehovah to afflict Job in order to demonstrate to the unseen powers the faith of the man. But this must not for a moment be supposed to convey any suggestion as to the real meaning of pain. So to read it is to misconceive the object of the prologue, and to set one's feet from the beginning on a path which is bound to lead to misunderstanding of *Job*. Davidson's language is unfortunate: "Does then the author offer no solution? He does not, and no solution is offered to us, unless the prologue supplies it. This passage, however, when naturally read, teaches that Job's sufferings were the trial of his righteousness." The prologue was not intended, to teach this or anything else. This is only the *machinery* of the drama, the author's way of getting his characters upon the stage and into action.

The meaning of suffering and its place in the providence of God are yet to seek. The methods of our author are those of the much decried "negative criticism"; but, for once at least in the history of "rationalism," his conclusions are wholly spiritual, and the total net result is not the destruction but the restoration of faith.

---

1. James Anthony Froude, *Short Studies on Great Subjects*, voI. i.
2. Carlyle, *On Heroes*: Lecture 2, "The Hero as Prophet."
3. A. B. Davidson, *Job* in the "Cambridge Bible for Schools"; and article *"Job"* in the *Encyclopedia Britannica,* eleventh edition.
4. W. T. Davison, article "Job" in Hastings' *Dictionary of the Bible*.
5. Froude, *Short Studies*.
6. Psalm xxxvii. 1-8.
7. Psalm lxxiii. 16.

CHAPTER 2
THE RESTORATION OF FAITH

The author permits us to see the restoration of faith in a fourfold vision.

1. GOD IN THE SOUL OF MAN.

In *Job* we have a picture, without question the noblest in literature, of a tried and suffering man who, in defiance of poverty, torture, and death, in defiance of all the thought and all the belief of all his world, and in defiance of Almighty God, will hold on to the integrity of his soul.

In defiance of God Himself!—that is the point. The martyrology of every nation is crowded with stories of men and women who have laughed to scorn the throned tyrannies of the world. It is crowded with the records of men and women who have opposed their death-defying "Credo" to the orthodoxies of the ages, backed by thumbscrew, rack, and gallows, by the legions and the gods and all the powers of hell. But these heroic souls had God on their side—and they knew it I Though for His purposes He suffered the forces of darkness for a time to wreak their will on the bodies of men and women who believed in His name, their souls were at peace with Him; and age by age they suffered the last pang of physical pain intensified to agony, and went to their God with a sigh of relief which was a prayer of faith, "Father, into Thy hand I commend my spirit."[1] Job has his martyrdom to endure unconsoled by any such faith. He opposes himself to the thought of his world as the martyrs of the Christian Church have done. He opposes himself to the leaders of the Church of his day as the martyrs have done. But, as they have not done, he nerves his soul to be true to the truth he knows is true, in defiance of what he yet believes is God!

The key-note of this heroic mood is found in one of the most famous passages in Job, one of the most famous in any literature and in any language of the world. "Though He slay me, yet will I trust Him," the passage used to read, falsifying the thought of Job and obscuring the greatest utterance of the poet. When the Revised Version gave a better translation devout persons read it with a sense of loss. "Foolish men, and slow of heart"—the new reading lights up the whole story of Job:

"Behold, He will slay me; I have no hope:
Nevertheless will I maintain my ways before
   Him."

He may slay me: God Himself may make war upon me. But this one thing God cannot do, He cannot make right wrong nor with the universe to back Him coerce me into a confession of a guilt I do not feel!

Seneca puts upon the lips of a pilot a sentiment only less noble: "O Neptune, you. may save me if you will; you may sink me if you choose; but whatever happens I shall hold my rudder true." Remember that this pilot believed in Neptune and in his power to sink or save; that he felt himself to be at that moment and throughout his life at Neptune's mercy; then seek to measure the immeasurable daring of this high resolve.

There is one spirit in these two brave sentences. It is the assertion of a reality more important and more lasting than what men call life, greater and more commanding than what men call God. In the Pilot it is proud loyalty to duty; in Job proud loyalty to truth. In both it is the assurance of a somewhat beyond all known and knowable things, something which is spirit and which is life.

Tennyson, in one of his shorter pieces, tells the story of a man who had lost faith in religion. His disordered mind had fed upon the crudest presentations of Calvinism and the cheapest utterances of

Atheism until he had come to hate the very thought of God. With his wife he seeks to drown himself. She is lost, he is rescued; and he wails out his anguish in blasphemies too sincere and despairing to be blasphemous. And even then he conceives of the possibility of God, the true God, the God whom Jesus called Father, the God of Love in whom we live and move and have our being.

> "What! I should call on that Infinite Lore
>   that has served us so well?
> Infinite cruelty rather that made everlasting
>   hell,
> Made us, foreknew us, foredoom'd us, and
>   does what He will with His own;
> Better our dead brute mother who never has
>   heard us groan!
>
> Hell? if the souls of men were immortal, as
>   men have been told,
> The lecher would cleave to his lusts, and the
>   miser would yearn for his gold,
> And so there were hell for ever! but were
>   there a God as you say,
> His love would have power over hell till it
>   utterly vanish'd away.
>
> And yet—I have had some glimmer at times,
>   in my gloomiest woe,

> Of a God behind all—after all—the great
>   God for aught that I know;
> But the God of Love and of hell together—
>   they cannot be thought.
> If there be such a God, may the Great God
>   curse him and bring him to nought!"
>
> — TENNYSON, *DESPAIR*.

When Tennyson wrote this he had eighteen centuries of Christian thinking in his blood, and for eighteen centuries the Spirit of Christ had been modifying the air he breathed. The author of *Job* conceived of this God, behind all, after all, the great God whom he did not know, long ages before the only begotten Son who was in the bosom of' the Father declared Him. Flesh and blood did not reveal this unto him. But the Spirit of the living God gave him understanding. And he appealed away from the God of all the orthodoxies upon earth to the God enthroned within his soul.

2. THE GOD ABOVE ALL.

Job's appeal is not in vain. It is to -carry him far. It is to bring him within sight of the reality to which he cries, and here, as everywhere, wisdom is justified of her children. "I will not believe," says Sir Oliver Lodge, "that it is given to man to think out a clear and consistent system higher and nobler than the real truth. Our highest thoughts are likely to be nearest to reality." The man of science in the twentieth century re-phrases the conviction which our old-world poet voices in undying tones. The modern thinker shapes and formulates the instinctive reaching out of the spirit of this prophetic man. The author of *Job* first conceives of the possibility that such a God might be, and on this God he calls. Then he comes to feel that this possible, conceivable God is God, the true God, and that God will do him right.

More than once Job utters this personal, deathless faith in a personal, changeless God. Twice he pours out the passion of his soul in matchless words which the world will never let die. From the abysses of despair, when it seems to himself that he has been "broken in pieces," he rises upon the wings of hope to heights of unsurpassable 'assurance which are to this day the crown and climax of believing prayer, and which must remain the joy of faithful hearts for ever.

> "But as for me I know that my Vindicator[2]
>   liveth,
> And at last He will stand up upon the earth:
> And after my skin, even this body, is destroyed,
> Then without my flesh shall I see God;
> Whom I, even I, shall see on my side."
>
> —JOB XIX. 25-27.

If he cannot abide permanently on these heights, if the impious piety of his friends drags him down from them, his dauntless spirit seeks them again, and again ascends them. He cannot see God, but he longs for Him, and he is sure of Him.

> "Oh that I knew where I might find Him!
> That I might come even to His seat!
> I would set my cause in order before Him,
> And fill my mouth with arguments.
> I would know the words which He would
>   answer me,
> And understand what He would say
>   unto me.
> Would He contend with me in the greatness
>   of His power?
> Nay; but He would give heed unto me.
> There the upright might reason with Him;
> So should I be delivered for ever from my
>   judge.
> Behold, I go forward, but He is not there;
> And backward, but I cannot perceive Him;
> On the left hand, when He doth work, but I
>   cannot behold Him;
> He hideth Himself on the right hand, that I
>   cannot see Him.
> But He knoweth the way that I take;
> When He hath tried me, I shall come forth as
>   gold."

—JOB XXIII. 3-10.

3. THE REAL REWARDS OR RIGHTEOUSNESS.

One great truth slowly emerges as the drama of Job unfolds. The rewards of righteousness are not to be found in material things, not in flocks of sheep and herds of cattle, and droves of camels, not in stocks and bonds and bank balances, and they must not be sought there. From this point of view the epilogue adds nothing to the grandeur of the poem, and it represents only a lower conception of dramatic completeness. The rewards of righteousness are in these convictions which we have been discussing, the integrity of the soul, the conscious appeal from earth to heaven, and the realised presence of God our Saviour. You shall not translate "Good" as "Goods"; you shall not measure by the stature of material things nor by the standard of the market, for this is a standard which God has rejected.[3] But the sense of work well done, and a heart at rest with itself, and the answer of a quiet conscience, and the love of men and women you have served and saved, and the smiles of little children, and joy and peace in the Holy Spirit, these are the rewards of righteousness, and these cannot be taken from you by any force or fraud, by fire or calamity or death. And this is why Luther's words, done by Carlyle into English as mighty as Luther's German, are true and righteous altogether —

> "And though they take our life,
> Goods, honour, children, wife;
> Yet is their profit small,
> These things shall perish all;
> The city of God remaineth."
>
> —1 SAMUEL XVI.7.

4. ULTIMA VERITAS.

But the last of these great truths which are interwoven with the very fabric of the Book of Job remains to be stated. And how simple it is, how elementary—yet how profound, overwhelming, eternal! When we cannot know, it is enough to trust, and when we cannot understand we shall be saved from darkness and despair if we can only love. We must all be agnostics somewhere, if only we will put our agnosticism in the right place. A little insight into the character of God may be infinitely more helpful to us than much foresight of His purposes. In the hour when terrors threaten we have but to stand still and see the glory of the Lord. And when the clouds are so thick that no glory can break through the gloom, all the wisdom of all the ages is in the counsel to trust in the Lord and wait patiently for Him. What availed the speculations, protestations, and fulminations of Job in the end? They had but darkened counsel by words without knowledge. Job had heard of Jehovah by the hearing of the ear. But when his heart saw the living God he was content. This is the truth of truths, the first truth and the last, that

> "Somewhere beyond the stars
>   Is a Love that is better than fate:
> When the night unlocks her bars
>   I shall see Him, and I will wait."
>
> — WASHINGTON GLADDEN, *ULTIMA VERITAS.*

---

1. For instances of martyrs and famous leaders of the Church dying with these words on their lips, see Prothero, *The Psalms in Human Life.*
2. "Redeemer" in the text, "Vindicator" in the margin.
3. 1 Samuel xvi. 7.

CHAPTER 3
SATAN IN LITERATURE AND IN LIFE

An exposition of the "Satan" of the Book of Job can never be entirely satisfactory, and for these reasons:

First, the author assumes as matters of common knowledge things about which we have little or no information.

Second, we are not sufficiently certain of the date of *Job* to find the needed information in contemporary literature and life, in the theology, traditions, and folk-lore of the time.

Third, the pictoral representation of the unseen powers of the universe, the personifications which our author employs, the actions and motives which he ascribes to the "spiritual hosts" alike of "wickedness"—if it be wickedness—and of holiness in "the heavenly places,"[1] are all so far removed from our habits of thought that we cannot attach reality to them. Only very radical treatment of the discussion can make possible dear thinking and spiritual edification. Yet we must be careful not to find in *Job* conceptions which may be entirely our own.

SATAN IN THE PROLOGUE.

Viewing the presentation of the Satan as we find it in the first two chapters of the Book of Job these things appear:—

1. Satan presents himself in the court of Heaven along with the sons of God. There is no definition of terms. We are not told who the sons of God are. We are not told how Satan comes to be numbered with them yet to be different from them. His name is best defined as "the adversary," though of what or of whom he is the adversary, or why as the adversary he should be present in the court of Heaven, is not dearly stated.

2. There is no hostility between the Satan and Jehovah. There is no rebellion, no disobedience on the part of Satan, no rebuke addressed by Jehovah to him. He is received on equal terms with the sons of God. He appears to be himself one of the sons of God. They seem to have been busy about Jehovah's business on earth, and the Satan appears to occupy a favoured and distinguished position amongst them. He is a sort of superintendent or inspector or overseer who, in the discharge of his duty to Jehovah, has been "going to and fro in the earth and walking

up and down in it" The sons of God, apparently, are reporting upon their work, and Satan reports on his. And he is interrogated by Jehovah concerning one great and notable personage on earth. Job, "the greatest of all the children of the east."

3. The Satan is authorised by Jehovah to do a definite work; he is instructed to apply burning tests to the man of Uz.

4. And in this connection it appears that he has power to inflict sufferings upon the race of men, or upon individual men. As we know, robbers from the desert carry away Job's possessions, his camels and his oxen; fire destroys his sheep; a great wind brings down the house in which his sons and daughters are gathered, and all ten perish in the ruins; and Job is brought near to death by a frightful disease. These things, we gather, are caused by the Satan. But all, it must be carefully noted, are authorised by Jehovah. Satan does not do these things out of a malevolent disposition, warring against God. His authority is a delegated authority. Jehovah has given him leave to organise this succession of calamities and sorrows.

5. Negatively, this also should be noted. The Satan of *Job* does not tempt. The tempting serpent of the Garden of Eden is not here, nor the tempting Satan of New Testament story. This Satan afflicts—by Jehovah's express authority, as we have seen—he does not assail the soul of man.

So far, the Satan acts only as an angel, i.e. a "messenger," of God, not as a fallen angel nor as an evil spirit. He is obedient and faithful. And whether this is or is not a credible representation of the unseen forces which help to shape the lives of men, at least it is not inconsistent or unintelligible.

But now the discussion is complicated and the author's meaning is obscured by the Satan's own words and by the spirit which suggests them. He resorts to insinuations against the individual, and he is guilty of blasphemy against the race.

INSINUATIONS AGAINST JOB.

"Doth Job fear God for nought?" the Satan demands; and it is the mean, odious suggestion which for long ages the world has agreed to call satanic. "Hast not thou made a hedge about him, and about his house, and about all that he hath, on every side? Thou hast blessed the work of his hands, and his substance is increased in the land. But put forth thy hand now, and touch all that he hath, and he will renounce thee to thy face."[2] Whether we understand "Satan" or not, the man who speaks and thinks in this way has become Satanic, and the mood in which this view of men and women, of their deeds and their motives, arises spontaneously and habitually, is simply "devilish." It is not the individual maligned who suffers; it is the one who can think and say these things. When a man can travel from Dan even to Beer-sheba in human life and find all barren, find only selfishness, meanness, intrigue, and calculating policy in the hearts of men and women, it is not the men and women who are wrong; it is his own "satanised" soul. Our world is full of human goodness and kindness. The atmosphere we breathe is charged with neighbourly helpfulness. It is not possible to name one known form of human weakness, sorrow, or distress remediable or capable of alleviation which men and women have not organised themselves to combat If to-day a new form of suffering were discovered, conceivably removable by the effort of pity, love, and generous help, to-morrow a "society" or "committee" would be formed to fight the cause and find the cure. In every town and village in the world men and women "serve God for nought"—save God alone!

BLASPHEMIES AGAINST THE RACE.

"All that a man hath will he give for his life"—God be praised, it is Satan's own lie! As these lines are being written there comes a pathetic, inspiring refutation of it. A friend of the writer, an English physician resident in San Francisco, has been bitten by a mad dog. Her Japanese "boy," a servant in her home, has been bitten, too. They are at this moment undergoing the Pasteur treatment. And the doctors cannot persuade the boy to take any food other than bread and water, though they tell him that he needs to "keep his strength up" with good nourishing food. But the boy says wearily—he has picked up the notion somewhere, perhaps in his home in Japan—that when one has been bitten by a rabid animal, if he eats nothing but bread and water, then, if he goes mad, "he will not bite anybody." And this splendid, ignorant boy, with the courage of a hero and the devotion of a saint, is jeopardising the success of the Pasteur treatment, running the risk, that is to say, of a hideous death from hydrophobia, so as not to risk the remote possibility of inflicting injury upon an unknown "somebody else" And the records of the Christian martyrs reveal no grander spirit All that a man hath he will give for his life? This Japanese servant will not give for his life the humanity which God has planted in his soul.

What is the great, outstanding marvel which stands revealed in every notable railway accident or wreck at sea or fire in a building crowded with human beings? Not the readiness on the part of some hero to throw his life away, in the attempt to save a man or woman strange to him; not the absolute certainty that there is one hero there; but the fact that this hero is of the same flesh and blood and human spirit as everybody else; that he has come out of the crowd and will fall back into the crowd; and that never spark leaps from the stroke of flint or steel more inevitably than sacrifice, chivalry, and heroism leap from the contact of this rugged soul with human need. The simple fact is that we are brave all our life without knowing it. It has become instinctive with us. There are thousands of years of hereditary courage in our blood. And of any blaspheming Satan of our day who asks us to believe that all that a man hath he will give for his life the words stand sure, "When he speaketh a lie, he speaketh of his own; for he is a liar, and the father thereof."[3]

SATAN IN WORLD-LITERATURE.

The poets are the truest interpreters of life. Three of the greatest of these children of genius have stamped upon the thought of the world their conception of the adversary—the opposing, tempting principle in the heart of man and in the universe.

Milton.

In Milton, Satan is one of the great angels of God. He revolts, tries to establish an independent kingdom, is overcome by God and flung into hell, with all his fellow traitors. In hell they set themselves to plan and carry on rebellion. They hear of a new world and of man, and they determine to invade it, feeling that they can either conquer it and live there instead of in hell, or ravage and waste it and so do injury to a province of their Almighty foe. Satan, therefore, is sent to reconnoitre and report. He finds out where earth is and goes; enters Eden, and hears the conversation between Adam and Eve. He sits by the side of the sleeping Eve, and in the shape of a toad tries to hiss evil thoughts through her ear into her mind. Ithuriel finds him there and forces him away. He returns in a mist, enters the serpent, accosts Eve and persuades her to eat of the forbidden fruit. Then Satan returns to hell, and there he and his followers are changed into serpents; trees spring up, laden with what seems delicious fruit, which, when they eat, turns to dust and ashes in their mouths. So has the bruising of the serpent's head already begun.

The point of this is that Milton's Satan becomes a Satan through baffled ambition and hateful self-love. He *will* win! He *must* triumph! He will gratify himself, his hate, his revenge, his mortified longing for self-glorification, utterly reckless of another's loss or sorrow, utterly reckless of the loss or sorrow of a world. *It is the typical crime of the universe.*

Byron.

In Byron, the devil finds Cain in an evil mood, discontented with his lot, hating work. He racks the mind of the man with questions of life, death, good, evil, which the man is incapable of answering, which, indeed, he is incapable of understanding. In his revolt against law and God his rage is enflamed; hate blazes up, and he becomes a murderer.

And again the lesson lies on the surface. Whatever may be the pressure of pain or the poignancy of thought rebellion will not help. We shall not make the burden lighter by raging against it To a brave heart and a joyous faith the perplexities and troubles of life one by one yield and bow—and if they do not disappear from the life which now we live, this same brave heart or joyous faith is assured that they are "a light affliction" and "for the moment," which is "working for us more and more exceedingly an eternal weight of glory."[4] And the warning of Byron's *Cain* is in the words which God Himself speaks to the first murderer while yet there is for him time to be wise, "Why art thou wroth, and why is thy countenance fallen? If thou doest well, shall it not be lifted up? But if thou doest not well, behold sin croucheth[5] at the door; and unto thee is its desire—but thou shouldst rule over it!"

Goethe.

The difference between Milton's "Satan" and Goethe's "Mephistopheles" is the difference between the primitive conceptions of an ancient people and the aspirations and yearnings of our complex civilisation. Mephistopheles is a sneering devil. Though a tempter, he tempts by scoffs. He finds his victim baffled in the search for knowledge, devitalised, and in that mood an easy prey.

It is when the higher faculties are wearied and the higher emotions are exhausted that we are ready to yield to the lower. The sins of saints are often no more than the actual devitalisation of the spiritual powers through excitement and overstrain. After spiritual triumph spiritual defeat is easy. But a soul is "lost" only when the higher is permanently subordinated to the lower. This is the sin unto death.[6] But it is not so with Faust. For conscience is at work. He is willing to risk his life to save his victim. There is something which he, too, will not "give for his life." And at last he is victorious in the discovery that only in working for the general good does man attain unto life.

To this conclusion come at last poetry, philosophy, and revelation. The Son of God is manifested to destroy the works of the devil.[7] And when Christ who is our life is manifested—in our life—then shall we also be manifested with Him in glory.[8]

---

1. Ephesians vi. 12.
2. Job i. 10, 11.
3. John viii. 44.
4. 2 Corinthians iv. 17.
5. Better than "coucheth": sin is a wild beast, crouching to make his spring. Genesis iv. 6, 7.
6. 1 John v. 16.
7. 1 John iii. 8.
8. Colossians iii. 4.

CHAPTER 4
ELIPHAZ THE SEER

The three friends who come to condole with Job are named Eliphaz, Bildad, and Zophar. The author means us to mark certain capital distinctions which separate any one of them from either of the other two. Sub-deties of characterisation are not to be looked for—at least, by the ordinary student reading the book in English. Broadly we may say that Eliphaz is a man of the old, prophetic type, if not quite great enough to be considered a prophet We will call him a seer. Bildad is a man wise with the lore of his time and[of preceding generations. We will call him' a sage. Zophar is the average religious man of his day, without distinguished intellectual or spiritual culture. And, without prejudice, he may be described as an ordinary soul.

The arrangement of the discussion is of primitive simplicity. There are three cycles of speeches.

The friends speak in turn, and Job replies to each before the other begins. In the third cycle Zophar does not speak—unless the disputed passage in chapter xxvii is his final word. So there are three speeches by Eliphaz with three replies by Job, three speeches by Bildad with three replies, and two speeches by Zophar with Job's replies. Eliphaz, clearly the oldest man of the three, the wisest, and the most important, is in all the cycles the first speaker.

THE FIRST SPEECH OF ELIPHAZ.

The opening words of Eliphaz breathe genuine sympathy and a spirit entirely noble. He grieves with Job in his grief. He appeals from Job in adversity to Job in prosperity, and exhorts his friend to recall his own teaching, and the faith which he had' preached to those in affliction. He plunges at once into an assertion of the law of life, as he and the other two understand it, and as he supposes Job understands it, the law of reward and retribution—an assertion which is to cause Job greater mental and spiritual suffering than the Satan has been able to inflict. But there is no bitterness and no condemnation in the words of Eliphaz nor in his thought. His meaning is, good must come to the upright man, evil to the bad man: you have been upright; take courage, therefore, and look for a good issue from all.

But the word "upright" as applied to any human being, and every related and similar word connoting righteousness, must be regarded as subject to a thousand deductions and qualifications. Eliphaz shrinks from the implication of his own words. And he proceeds to affirm the corruption of our human nature in round set speech which leaves no loophole for exception. In language, the majesty of which has appealed to every person of literary taste who has ever opened the Book of Job, Eliphaz describes his vision in the night:

> "Fear came upon me, and trembling.
> Which made all my bones to shake.
> Then a spirit passed before my face;
> The hair of my flesh stood up.
> It stood still, but I could not discern the appearance thereof;
> A form was before mine eyes;
> There was silence, and I heard a voice, saying,
> Shall mortal man be just before God?
> Shall a man be pure in the presence of his Maker?"
>
> — JOB IV. 14-17.

It is pathetic to reflect that the vision of Eliphaz, so awe-inspiring in itself, and described in language the most impressive which has ever served to make an apparition real, does but bring to him a supernatural sanction of his disheartening dogma concerning the corruption of mankind!

But clearly it is not for Job to storm the battlements of heaven with his audacities. Man does but suffer the consequences of this frailty of his blood. Virtue consists in submission to the will of God. God is righteous, and His beneficence is over all. Were he, Eliphaz, in like manner afflicted he would seek unto God, humbly, penitently, dutifully; he would praise Him for His providence, His goodness, and His unceasing care. Yea, he would go further; he would praise Him for His chastisements—"happy is the man whom God correcteth"—and to this submission he exhorts Job, promising to him, in the name of his God, deliverance from all his trouble, the restoration of his wealth, children and children's children, a grand old age, a sweet and peaceful death.

THE FAILURE OF THE SPEECH.

The speech fails of its purpose. Examining it carefully we see that it was bound to fail.

The speech lacks the note of human feeling. In the common phrase of our day, there is no red blood in it. Lofty? Yes. Eloquent? Without a doubt. And true as the truth was then conceived. For us the theology is bad theology and the philosophy is unsound. And this, we know, is the view of the author. He allows the patriarch to put the friends to silence.

Jehovah rebukes them. These facts must be borne in mind throughout the study of *Job*. It would be wearying to insist upon them at each fresh stage of the debate. The point, however, is not that the theology and the philosophy are false and bad, but that theology and philosophy, good or bad, are wholly out of place. At such an hour it is not loftiness of thought nor eloquence of diction nor the most admired truths of philosophy which the sufferer needs. He wants the grip of a friend's hand, the light that shines from a soul that knows through eyes that see, and most of all, he wants to feel that his friend feels as he does—resents as a personal wrong the grief that has fallen upon him, and is ready when occasion offers to take up arms on his behalf against the universe l This may not be sound theology nor may it fit the mood of a great philosopher. But theology and philosophy are precisely what the sufferer cannot away with. He wants to feel the heart-beats of a brother man.

If the preacher is to bring to the sorrowing comfort and strength he must identify himself with his suffering brother. The successful advocate in a court of justice insists upon the "we" until one smiles at the affectation. But there is no madness in his method. "We" did this, he asserts, "we" said that, and "we" are ready to swear to something else. And the unsuccessful preacher says "you!" The difference too often is not in word; it is in the essence and in substance. A preacher cannot find for the word he speaks entrance into another's heart until he has knocked at the door of his own. He must bring to repentance the sinner in the pulpit before he can convict of sin the sinner in the pew. His deepest word must ever be, "Come and let us return unto the Lord!" "Let *us* exalt His name *together*!" And when he kneels by the bed of pain or stands with the bereaved by the open grave, he cannot mediate to the stricken soul the consolation of our God unless he first resents with a personal resentment the stroke which has fallen, and then along with the sufferer submits himself to the will of God. "When Jesus therefore saw her weeping, and the Jews also weeping who came with her, he was moved with indignation in the spirit, and was troubled."[1] We have not a high priest that cannot be touched with the feel of our infirmities!

THE SECOND SPEECH OF ELIPHAZ.

The faults of the first speech are accentuated in the second. And there is an added element of bitterness. Eliphaz has been deeply wounded by the contempt with which Job has brushed aside his philosophising and the preaching of his companions. He has lost patience with Job, and he shows it He is shocked and horrified by the daring irreverences of Job, the rebelliousness of his complaints and the audacity of his appeals to the Most High. And he is persuaded that Job is a worse man than he supposed. Sorrow and affliction are bringing the true man into view, Eliphaz thinks, and the true Job he begins to see in a very unfavourable light. Iniquity and craftiness, he declares, shape the thoughts of Job; and the words of his mouth condemn him. He comes back to his degrading view of human nature, once more affirming its innate corruption, and in support of his view appeals to the judgment of the pure races of mankind in many ages.

But in one way the matter of his polemic has been modified. He ceases to declare that all is well with the righteous; he contents himself with proclaiming the penal consequences of wrong-doing. It is a characteristic of the genius of our author that he puts into the mouth of Eliphaz large and striking truths concerning the fate of the wicked. When he asserts a law, a law which knows no exceptions and no delays, he is in error as to the fact. When he reverses the statement of the law, "The wicked suffer," and makes it read, "Those who suffer are wicked," he wrongs both man and God. When he applies the inverted rule to a particular instance, the case of Job, and asserts Job's gross and palpable wickedness, he himself descends to gross and palpable untruths. The things that he asserts concerning the retributive consequences of guilt are true, and we do well to remember them: the sense of threatening calamity induced by an accusing conscience, and the disintegrating, destructive power of sensual sin. It is the use he makes of these truths which turns them into cruel falsities. It is not enough to present the truth. The truth must be presented truly. God, justice, and Eternal Judgment, Christ, the Incarnation, and the Atonement, truths more indestructible than the universe, may each and every one of them be affirmed by the preacher in such a way as to be false to the mind or heart that needs them most. We need to remember that every apologetic, like every appeal, is relative—it is relative to the individual to whom it is addressed, and relative as well to his temperament, his circumstances, and the mood in which it finds him.

Eliphaz concludes without a word of sympathy, without a breath of hope. And such a conclusion condemns itself.

THE THIRD SPEECH OF ELIPHAZ.

When next Eliphaz speaks it is clear that his thoughts have gone from bad to worse. The lesson of it has been admirably stated: "In this last colloquy we are saddened by an impressive illustration of the baneful effect of mere controversy even on a mind of the largest and most generous kind. Eliphaz, the prophet, sinks well-nigh to the level of Zophar, the bigot. . . . Stung by the mortification of defeat, he breaks out into a string of definite charges against Job, accusing him of the most vulgar and brutal crimes for which he could allege no shadow of proof."[2]

The language is not too strong. Eliphaz is not satisfied with hints of secret wrongdoing. He is not content with the assertion of his false and foolish syllogism: "The wicked suffer; you are suffering; therefore you are wicked." He comes down to particulars, and lies—there is no other word for it—for the honour of God, as many have done since, but never without disaster;

> "For thou hast taken pledges of thy brother for nought,
> And stripped the naked of their clothing.
> Thou hast not given water to the weary to drink,
> And thou hast withholden bread from the hungry.
> Thou hast sent widows away empty,
> And the arms of the fatherless have been broken."
>
> —JOB XXII. 6, 7, 9.

There can be no palliation of this. We had better learn the lesson of it. That lesson is "writ large" across the history of councils, synods, assemblies for nearly twenty centuries. From theological bitterness to false witness against one's neighbour, how easy the descent! But when an honest difference of opinion about the meaning of a Hebrew verb or Greek substantive becomes an occasion of moral offence and a cause of rancour, of envy, hatred, malice, and all uncharitableness, the grounds of sanity have been departed from not less surely than the Christian spirit. Where there is no sense of proportion there is no sanity. And if any man have not the mind of Christ he is none of His!

THE SALVATION OR ELIPHAZ.

Most happily, in the case of Eliphaz, we have not to leave it here. The great man in him asserts itself above the cramping littleness of his creed. The soul of the seer sees and the heart of the prophet flames with love and truth. His final words are words of appeal, and the appeal is of all but matchless worth.

> "Acquaint now thyself with him and be at peace";

he begins, and in words of strength and grace and beauty he proceeds to tell the blessedness of the life which is lived in God. He speaks of its joy:

> "Thou shalt delight thyself in the Almighty";

of its assurance:

> "Thou shalt lift up thy face unto God";

of communion:

"Thou shalt make thy prayer unto him, and
    he will hear thee";

of enduring influence:

"Thou shalt decree a thing and it shall be established unto thee;
And light shall shine upon thy ways";

and of the priesthood of believing souls:

"Even him that is not innocent thou shalt
    deliver;
Yea, he shall be delivered through the cleanness of thy hands."

Eliphaz has lost the debate, but he has saved—himself!

---

1. John xi. 33
2. Cox, *Job, in loco.*

CHAPTER 5
BILDAD THE SAGE

The first speech of Bildad is given in the eighth chapter of Job. It opens with a rebuke of the sufferer's stormy words (ver. 2), and proceeds at once to affirm the rectitude of all God's judgments (ver. 3). Bildad is harsh, cruelly harsh, from the outset He tells the bereaved father, in round, set terms, that his dead children deserved their fate (ver. 4); and after such an opening it is in vain that he exhorts Job to penitence and prayer (ver. 5). Yet in the spirit of many an unconvincing, unpersuasive preacher who thinks to scold a congregation into well-doing, Bildad holds his course. He claims the authority of the ages for his view. These are early days for an appeal to "the general consent of mankind," but we find it here, or at least, to the general consent of the wise and the learned of other generations. Verse 9 must not be quoted as a description of the awful brevity of our life upon the earth:

> "For we are but of yesterday and know
>   nothing,
> And our days upon the earth are as a
>   shadow."

Bildad means that it might be permissible for Job to consider his wisdom and the wisdom of the other two friends as of small account; that if it stood alone it would be of little worth, for they are children of their day and hour, living their little life and passing out of the sun. But the word which they speak is not theirs. It represents the garnered wisdom of ages—and of ages again. It is not the wisdom only of their fathers, but of their fathers' fathers (ver. 8), and it rests upon the experiences of uncounted centuries.

BILDAD'S SECOND SPEECH.

Bildad's second speech (chapter xviii) seems to possess no single redeeming quality. The first does make an attempt—a poor attempt, but still an honest one—to strike a note of hope:

> "Behold, God will not cast away a perfect
>   man,
> Neither will He uphold the evil-doers.

He will yet fill thy mouth with laughter,
And thy lips with shouting" —

if, it is understood, thou dost turn to Him and repent and acknowledge thy wickedness before Him. But now Bildad is incapable of even such poor preaching as this. With him, as with Eliphaz, personal resentment has bred bitterness of spirit, and Job's theological transgressions have assumed the dimensions of a huge moral wrong. Chapter xviii is a masterpiece in its way, and it is a pity that we are not free to admire its literary art and power. We feel with Job as well as for him, and like him we are angry that Bildad should say such things as these. But how well he says them! How finely he demands whether the eternal order shall be shaken to its depths to meet Job's necessities:

"Thou that tea rest thyself in thine anger,
Shall the earth be forsaken for thee?
Or the rock be removed out of its place?"

And his picture of the unrighteous man alone with his unrighteousness in the darkness of the night:

"Yea, the light of the wicked shall be put out,
And the spark of his fire shall not shine.
The light shall be dark in his tent,
And his lamp above him shall be put out."

With what art he accumulates synonyms for "net" in the famous passage which has driven one expositor to call this the "Net" speech:

"For he is cast into a net by his own feet,
And he walketh upon the *toils*.
A *gin* shall take him by the heel,
And a *snare* shall lay hold on him.
A noose is hid for him in the ground,
And a *trap* for him in the way."

And the climax to which he mounts, the *underlining* of his emphasis, so to speak:

"Surely such are the dwellings of the unrighteous,
And this is the place of him that knoweth not God."

He has cast very wide the net, the toils, the gin, the snare, the noose, and the trap of his rhetoric, and Job is finely caught within it!

THE THIRD SPEECH OR BILDAD.

There is nothing in Bildad's last word (chapter xxv). He stands amazed at the sight of Job's unsubduable irreverence. He gasps out a repetition of the Eliphaz contempt for human nature, protests that in the presence of the Ineffable there is no brightness in the moon and that the stars forget their shining; and so measuring the immeasurable distances between the holiness of God and the meanness of man "that is a worm" (ver. 6), turns away in shocked and stunned and solemn silence.

DEFENCES OF CLAY.

So, then, Bildad, the sage, adds nothing to the case presented by Eliphaz, the seer. His argument is the same: God punishes the wicked and rewards the righteous; Job is being punished for his wickedness; and it is impious to rebel against God. The falsity of the statement about Job and the fallacy of the argument are alike clear to us. And it would be a weariness to the flesh to analyse Bildad's speeches and point out their failures of logic and of humanity. When we seriously consider the paucity of the argument, the monotonous iteration and reiteration of the single, unsustained ' or badly sustained thesis, we are driven to the conclusion that so supreme an artist as the author of *Job* meant us to become intolerant, even a little disdainful, of their "memorable sayings" which Job denounced as "proverbs of ashes," and their dialectical defences which he scorned as "defences of clay."[1] In the case of Bildad, indeed, there is no claim to originality. Eliphaz appeals to visions of the night, Bildad only to the wisdom, of ages dead and gone. He is of the type of the scribe with whom study of the New Testament has made us familiar. His strength is grounded in precedent, authority, and antiquity. Men have always believed that God's judgments are such as he, Bildad, declares them to be; and who is Job that he should doubt it?

THE APPEAL TO ANTIQUITY.

Herein this ancient document is painfully modern. The mind that seeks strength and wisdom in the past, that contemns the present, and fears the future, is found in our day as in every day of which the record remains. "Conservative" and "Radical" are not theological terms, or words borrowed from party politics, nor even descriptions of antagonistic temperaments. They are terms of biology, and they go back to characteristics which were functional in protoplasm! The deadly offence of Socrates is that he does not "believe in the gods of the city," and that he "introduces new divinities." Aristophanes hates with a perfect hatred the "modernity" of the fifth century before Christ. The *Clouds* is his protest against the immorality of modern thought. His spirit is stirred within him when he contrasts the degeneracy of manners in his day with the simplicity and strength of life in the good old times of the Persian wars! The American housewife who complains of her "hired girl," and the English-woman who laments the eccentricities of her "maid," are not any more modern than that unpleasant Old Testament person who gave his opinion of "servants nowadays."[2] When Gladstone was a candidate for Newark—a young man of twenty-three—he was asked to explain what he meant by a sentence in his address about a "return to sounder general principles," and he replied that he had in mind "the manly and God-fearing principles of two hundred years before." The definiteness of his reply was unfortunate, for a mocking voice rang out, "when they burned witches!" Yet to minds so constituted as those of Aristophanes, Nabal, and Gladstone—and it would not be possible to name in one breath three individuals more widely separated by oceans of spiritual and temperamental differences—an appeal to the judgment of past times will always seem right and wise.

Oliver Wendell Holmes, with malice aforethought, puts the objection to this appeal in its crudest form. When Calvin and his associates made themselves a party to the burning of Servetus, the "Professor" declares that they were "in a state of religious barbarism"; and he goes on, "the dogmas of such people about the Father of mankind and His creatures are of no more account in my opinion than those of a council of Aztecs. If a man picks your pocket, do you not consider him thereby disqualified to pronounce any authoritative opinion on matters of ethics? If a man hangs my ancient female relative for sorcery, as they did in this neighbourhood a little while ago, or burns my instructor for not believing as he does, I care no more for his religious edicts than I should for those of any other barbarian."³

Between these two methods of regarding life the student of the Book of Job will hardly be called upon to choose. The choice has long ago been made, largely for him, partly by him. He will esteem the appeal to the past as of great or little worth according as his temperamental inclination is, to quote Oliver Wendell Holmes again, "toward God in us or God in our masters." But the age we live in, with its crying needs, bids the preacher believe that God is not a God of the dead but of the living, and demands of him whether he has not received the Holy Ghost since he believed. And Dr. Faunce, in his noble Yale lectures of 1908, goes so far as to assert that the whole discussion of the minister's mediating work may be summed up by saying that "he is to keep alive man's faith in an ever present God." He quotes the title of a story by Rudyard Kipling, *The Man who was*, and he says, "there are sincerely devout men who seem to believe in a God who was. He was with Moses, they say, opening up streams in the flinty rock; but now men must dig wells or build aqueducts if they want water. He was with Israel, granting the people bread from heaven; but now if a man wants bread, let him work for it. He was with David and anointed him to the kingship; but now he anoints nobody, and those who want high office must secure the votes. About the year 100 A.D. all inspiration ceased, and about 200 A.D. all miracles ceased, and now in a world bereft of divine voices we stumble and grope till the end. O young prophets of the truth, such an idea is the master falsehood of humanity! It is the one fundamental untruth which will put unreality into every sermon and impiety into every prayer. Our God was, and is, and is to come."[4]

---

1. Job xiii. 12.
2. 1 Samuel xxv. 10.
3. Oliver Wendell Holmes, *The Professor at the Breakfast Table*.
4. William H. P. Faunce, *The Educational Ideal in the Ministry*.

CHAPTER 6
ZOPHAR THE ORDINARY SOUL

Zophar is the last speaker in each of the first two cycles. In the third he does not appear. It is reasonable to suppose that he is the youngest of the three friends and the least important. But it must be remembered that all three are great men, representative of what is wisest and best in the life of their day and country. Job is a man "born out of due season," a man in advance of his time, a path-finder and a banner-bearer. In their eyes he is worse than an innovator. He is an iconoclast He is irreverent, profane, a blasphemer whose sufferings are the result of sin and the cause of deeper sin. We know that the friends are deeply in error. Jehovah testifies that they have said of Him the things which are not right But they are wise with the wisdom of their time. And they thought they did God service.

All this must be remembered as we come to the study of Zophar. He is not a man to be despised, however much we may, on Job's behalf, resent the things he says. He is not a seer like Eliphaz, nor a sage like Bildad; but the Church must have its ordinary souls as well as its seers and sages, its heroes and saints. If the things that he says are not new, at least he says them marvellously well, and some it would be difficult even now for any of us to say better. What can be liner than his outburst of wonder and awe in the presence of the divine omniscience?

> "Canst thou by searching find out God?
> Canst thou find out the Almighty unto perfection?
> It is high as heaven; what canst thou do?
> Deeper than Sheol; what canst thou know?"
>
> —JOB XI. 7, 8.

The man through whose lips the author of *Job* speaks these noble lines is not to be dismissed as a contemptible person noticeable only by reason of his odious vulgarity and bigotry.[1]

ZOPHAR'S FIRST SPEECH.

Zophar's opening words (chap. xi. vers. 1-6) cannot be defended. He is harsh from the very outset. He comes as a friend: he speaks as a foe. Read even in English his words have the effect of shots from a quick-firing gun. Job is a "babbler," a man "full of talk," literally "a man of lips" whose wild words come neither from brain nor heart, a "boaster" and a "mocker." Job has longed to hear God speak, but Zophar is satisfied that if Job should find himself cursed by the burden of a granted prayer he would be exposed and abased.

There follows the glowing tribute to the unspeakable wisdom of God already quoted, and then preaching which shows that this average man of a forgotten day has learned what we need always to remember that there is no "evangel" except preaching with promise. He exhorts Job (vers. 13, 14) to "set the heart right" and "stretch out the hands" to God. He bids him —

> "If iniquity be in thy hand, put it far away,
> And let not unrighteousness dwell in thy tents."

And if he will do this,

> "Surely then shalt thou lift up thy face without spot;
> Yea, thou shalt be steadfast, and shalt not fear:
> For thou shalt forget thy misery;

> Thou shalt remember it as waters that are
>   passed away.
> And thy life shall be clearer than the
>   noonday;
> Though there be darkness, it shall be as the
>   morning.
> And thou shalt be secure, because there is
>   hope;
> Yea, thou shalt search about thee, and shalt
>   take thy rest in safety.
> Also thou shalt lie down, and none shall
>   make thee afraid."
>
>   —JOB XI. 15-19.

He has spoken well, once the harshness of his opening words has been laid aside. The pity is that he should have prejudiced us against his message by the bitterness of his spirit. Herein is matter of grave concern. The preacher who "nags" is not by any means more admirable than the "nagging" husband or the "nagging" wife. It is depressing to "worship" in an atmosphere of fault-finding. It is intolerable to live in an atmosphere of "snarl." We cannot denounce people into goodness. We cannot coerce them to Christ. There are times when the world needs a son of thunder with his fiery tongue and prophet's heart of flame. But not all of us are called to an apostolate of protest or ministry of rebuke. Not all of us are fitted for it. The mighty hater may be a servant of God—but only on condition that he has first proved himself a heroic lover. The ethics of denunciation must be studied with greater care than we have yet bestowed upon it. Hate is too precious a thing to be wasted. It must be kept for the supreme moment and the Christ-like mood.[2] The Angel of the Church at Ephesus is praised because he hates "the works of the Nicolaitans, which I also hate." If we hate nothing which we are satisfied the Risen Christ does not hate we shall not go far wrong. And even then our "hate" must be so pure, so white-hot in its holiness, that it can live side by side with a love like His.

ZOPHAR'S SECOND SPEECH.

Zophar's second speech (chapter xx) passes all bounds. It follows close upon the marvellous appeal of Job from the injustice of earth to the justice of heaven. It is Zophar's coarse and cruel reply to Job's passionate "I know that my Vindicator liveth," and his assurance that his cause will triumph after his death. Zophar bids him believe (ver. 5) that "the triumph of the wicked is short" and the "joy of the godless for a moment" To us who know the facts Zophar's description of Job as an epicure in sin is merely foolish. To Job himself, sick in body and in mind and heart-sick, too, bereaved, abandoned, such wild and wicked charges are maddening. They lash his spirit. Zophar rushes on (vers. 12, 13):

> "Though wickedness be sweet in his mouth.
> Though he hide it under his tongue,
> Though he spare it, and will not let it go,
> But keep it still within his mouth"

rolls it under his tongue, that is to say, as a sweet morsel, this sin in which he delights!

No wonder Job refuses to recognise himself in so monstrous a description. "Hast thou considered my servant Job?"—we have not forgotten Jehovah's question, nor His account of die man of Uz: "There is none like him in the earth, a perfect and upright man, one that feareth God, and turneth away from evil"—not one that "sups full of horrors" and of infamies until the surfeit of them nauseates him (ver. 15)! Has Job challenged the verdict of heaven? Heaven and earth alike condemn him, Zophar says:

> "The heavens shall reveal his iniquity,
> And the earth shall rise up against him."

And once again, lest any should miss the personal application of all this, the formula is spoken:

> "This is the portion of a wicked man
>   from God,

And the heritage appointed unto him by
God."

GOSPEL-HARDENED.

We know that Job's daring and glorious appeal did not fail in heaven. It is painful to observe how it failed on earth. Coarseness and cruelty, we have seen, are Zophar's answer to the "Vindicator" passage—and not only to that immortal plaint but to a cry as sad, as heavily charged with anquish, as ever broke from a suffering heart:

"Have pity upon me, have pity upon me, O ye
my friends?
For the hand of God hath touched me."

—JOB XIX. 21.

How can this human nature of ours be so *in*-human, so callous, so wolfish? There is no answer to such a question. It is the tragedy of all redemptive work amongst men. It is the tragedy of Redemption. "What hast thou done?" Pilate demanded of the pale Prisoner at his judgment bar. And the answer might have been: Deeds of love and mercy without end! He was Pity incarnate, He was divine Compassion, He was ineffable Goodness and Gentleness. But priests conspired His death; the crowd clamoured for Barabbas; the soldiers lashed Him with whips, played a hideous game with Him as they blindfolded Him and demanded, "Prophesy who struck thee," pressed thorns upon His brow—and they crucified Him! Age by age the terribly sad word of Isaiah, quoted by Jesus, quoted again by Paul, has been fulfilled in the lives of men and women.[3] They have grown harder and coarser, as the word of God has been proclaimed to them. The heart has become fat, and the ears heavy, and their eyes have been closed. Browning attempts an answer to Shakespeare's question:

> "'Is there a reason in nature for these hard
>   hearts!' O Lear,
> That a reason out of nature must turn them
>   soft, seems clear";

but the horror of great darkness falls upon us when we discover that the "reason out of nature" incarnate in the Son of God fails at times to "turn them soft."

In a way there is a measure of sad comfort for the preacher in a remembrance of these facts. We fail. Our preaching fails. Our prayers fail. The man or woman we have agonised for lives in sin and dies in sin. And we reproach ourselves with the failure and say that if we had lived nearer to God and with an importunity of prayer that would not be denied besought Him for this life, the effectual fervent prayer would not have returned unto us void. Yes, perhaps, in some particular case. But Isaiah knew that failure was sometimes inevitable, and Paul knew it; and our Lord affirmed that such experiences partake of the nature of law. These things are too high for us; we turn away from them with a heavy heart. But the measure of self-blame is reduced, and each of us is able to find relief in the reflection,

> "   I am glad to think
> I am not bound to make the world go right;
> But only to discover and to do.
> With cheerful heart, the work that God
>   appoints.
>   I will trust' in Him
> That He can hold His own."
>
> — JEAN INGELOW.

THE TRIPLE BLUNDER.

Now that the speeches of Eliphaz, Bildad, and Zophar are before us, it is easy to see the rocks on which each went to grief. We may speak of a "triple blunder" and be twice right, for each one of the three is guilty of the same three mistakes, any one of which would have made shipwreck of intentions as good as theirs.

1. Personal resentment warps their views. It must ever be remembered that they come to Job with honest hearts, anti that they speak to him the

things which they sincerely believe. Job has been their friend. They have honoured and loved him. We shall lose half the value of *Job* if we forget this. When he takes the course along which they vainly try, for a time at least, to follow him, they are surprised, grieved, overwhelmed. They remonstrate in all singleness of purpose, thinking they do God service. He takes their remonstrances in bad part, and for the reason we have seen: there was not enough of the milk of human kindness in the philosophy with which they sought to sustain his failing spirit. He replies to them, it must be admitted, roughly, contemptuously. From the first he is so hurt by their academic discussion of his sorrows that he does not once manifest gratitude for their visit or respect for themselves. And they allow themselves to be carried off their feet by chagrin, mortification, offended pride. They are carried out of themselves by these emotions. They cease to be theologians, philosophers, teachers of truth. They are merely very angry men who say things which are not only spiteful but silly.

It would not be superfluous to point the moral. The overseer of souls "must be without reproach . . . temperate, sober-minded, orderly . . . apt to teach, *no brawler*, no striker, but gentle, not contentious"[4] —in short, just such a one as neither Eliphaz nor Bildad has proved himself to be.

2. They fail to heed their own teaching. Through long speeches which for very weariness one for-

bears to quote they have declared that "God" is too vast a conception for the mind of the creature to grasp. It is not only Zophar who exclaims, "Heights of heaven, what canst thou do!" as he contemplates man's feeble attempt to express the infinite. The vision of Eliphaz deepens his intuitive conviction that man is insignificant in the presence of the Most High. And all the learning of Bildad does but confirm his belief that man is a worm.[5] Oh, the pity of it, the pity of it, the pity that they did not remember something of their over-great protesting! Then they might have bethought themselves of the possibility that in a scheme of things so vast, a universe of thought so truly immeasurable, controlled by a God whose thought can never be less than infinite, there might be room for theories or truths or facts and laws which they have not yet taken into account. It may be true, as Mr. Chesterton would have us believe, that the "I may be wrong" attitude of many a weakly apologetic soul is a blasphemy against the God within us and without. But unless the strong man is to become a brute, crushing human hearts beneath his knee of prayer, he must be willing to add to his assurance that "I am right" the large and luminous and beautiful belief that his neighbour who differs from him may be as right as he is! He must be ready, and not only ready but glad, to believe that there are still more things in heaven and earth than are dreamt of in his philosophy.

3. They allow their theories to over-ride their humanity.

Admitting that their theories are conscientiously held, ought they to treat a bereaved and suffering man, that man their friend, as they have done? If the reader is inclined to answer, "Starting from their premises they could do no other," he may well begin to ponder the entire problem of *Job* afresh. And the answer which the present writer suggests—and it is only a suggestion—may carry the thinker for. There are certain root-instincts of our human nature which are supreme over any theory of life no matter how intellectually conceived or conscientiously held. Davidson finds that under the first speech of Zophar lies the question, "If the affirmations of a man's conscience or of his consciousness be contradicted by the affirmations of God, what does it become a man to do?"[6] This question underlies every question in *Job*. It is the ground of the problem of *Job*. And Davidson says that it is wise in such a case to "raise the prior question,' Is this supposed affirmation of God really His affirmation?' or to raise the prior question on the other side, 'Is this affirmation of conscience, which seems opposed to the intimations of God, a true affirmation of conscience?'" This is wise, but when the prior question has been raised, and still the apparent contradiction waits, waits and will not go away, is theory (the "supposed affirmation of God") or what has just been termed "a root-instinct of our human nature" (the "supposed affirmation of conscience") to be given right of way? We shall be better and wiser men and women for believing that tenderness, sympathy, compassion, generosity, brotherly love, and a flaming pity will still be counted Godlike when every theory about them has crumbled into dust. "The heart has its reasons," and the fruit of the spirit is love, joy, peace, long-suffering, kindness, goodness, faithfulness, meekness, self-control; against such there is no "theory"—and no law.[7]

---

1. The reader who is interested may turn with profit to Cox's vituperative characterisation of Zophar in his commentary on Job; and then he should open Joseph Parker's People's Bible vol. i i, "Job" and note how Cox's denunciation of Zophar drove Parker into a eulogy of the " fearlessly critical deeply religious" Zophar more unreasonable than Cox's bitterness. It is more than entertaining. It is significant. To preachers it is a warning.
2. Frederick William Robertson relates a conversation in which he took part. Someone maintained that "the indignation expressed by Christ against hypocrisy was no precedent for us, inasmuch as He spoke as a Divine person." And Robertson goes on: "I contended that it was human, and if a man did not feel something of the same spirit under similar circumstances, if his blood could not boil with indignation, nor the syllable of withering justice rise to his lips, he could not even conceive His spirit. Mr. E agreed to this, to my surprise, and told an anecdote. 'Could you not have felt indignation for that, Robertson?' My blood was at the moment running fire—not at his story, however; and I remembered that I had once in my life stood before my fellow-creature with words that scathed and blasted; once in my life I felt a terrible might; I knew, and rejoiced to know, that I was in-

dicting the sentence of a coward's and a liar's hell."—*Life and Letters of the Rev. W. Robertson*, p. 141.
3. Isaiah vi. 9, 10. See George Adam Smith's wonderful note on this passage and his striking quotation from Mazzini.
4. 1 Timothy iii. 2, 3
5. Job xxv. 6.
6. A. B. Davidson, *Job*; comment on chapter xi.
7. Galatians v. 22, 23.

CHAPTER 7
THE INTERVENTION OF ELIHU

The three friends of Job have failed. They have failed to convict him of sin. They have failed to alleviate his grief. They have failed to justify the ways of God to men. The weakness of the case made out by them has become more and more apparent as the controversy has run on. This is the design of the author. He means us to see and feel that the older interpretations of the problem of pain break down as soon as they are brought to the test of detailed and careful examination. He succeeds perfectly in his intention.

He succeeds too well. The unsatisfactory nature of the speeches was just as obvious to Hebrew readers as it is to Christian. It was as clear to the third or fourth century B.C. as to the twentieth A.D. And some later author, of lower inspiration, boldly took upon himself to construct a stronger polemic.

He attempted to enter into the spirit of the drama. He created another character. He called him Elihu. He represented him as a deeply interested auditor who had listened with amazement and growing anger to the impotent discourses of the three friends. And he placed upon the lips of Elihu the arguments which, to his mind, come nearer to a solution of the problem than those advanced by Eliphaz, Bildad, and Zophar.[1]

THE CONTRIBUTION OF ELIHU.

Elihu is more than angry. "Then was kindled the wrath of Elihu . . . against Job was his wrath kindled . . . also against the three friends was his wrath kindled because they had found no answer" (chap, xxxii. 2, 3). He is a young man, and he explains that he has refrained from speech because of his youth, but he finds that it does not follow that the "great" are wise or that the aged understand justice (vers. 6-10). He has listened with what patience, with what show of respect was possible (vers. 11, 12); he has been amazed and humiliated by the dialectical victory which they have allowed Job to win (vers. 15, 16), and now he simply must speak:

> "For I am full of words;
> The spirit within me constraineth me.
> Behold, my breast is as wine which hath no
>   rent;

Like new wine-skins it is ready to burst."

— CHAP, XXXII. 18, 19.

He has no doubt of his own inspiration, none as to the finality of his great deliverances:

"The Spirit of God hath made me,
And the breath of the Almighty giveth me life.
If thou canst, answer thou me;
Set thy words in order before me, stand forth."

— CHAP, XXXIII. 4, 5.

And again:

"Suffer me a little, and I will show thee;
For I have yet somewhat to say on God's behalf.
I will fetch my knowledge from afar,
And will ascribe righteousness to my Maker.
For truly my words are not false;
One that is perfect in knowledge is with thee."

— CHAP, XXXVI. 2-4.

And throughout he speaks in the same tone.

We are bound to ask what contribution he makes to the discussion of the tremendous theme on which our minds are busy. And we find that he really is in possession of one great idea which the friends have not brought out with any distinctness. They have insisted that suffering is punishment, and that punishment is retributive. Elihu, not less convinced than they that suffering is punishment, holds that it may be and often is *curative*. The friends have all along maintained that such retributive punishment is compatible with the divine justice, is, indeed, demanded by it. Elihu affirms that it is compatible with divine love and tenderness, and is the outcome of these. He has earlier stated that God draws near to man in dreams and in visions of the night for the purpose of warning him against sin and deterring him from it.

> "In a dream, in a vision of the night,
> When deep sleep falleth upon men,
> In slumberings upon the bed;
> Then he openeth the ears of men,
> And sealeth their instruction,
> That he may withdraw man from his
>   purpose,
> And hide pride from man;
> He keepeth back his soul from the pit,
> And his life from perishing by the sword."
>
> — CHAP, XXXIII. 15-18.

This is a great conception, and it is rendered greater and more gracious by his belief that when such visions fail and the interpretation of them, when a man has gone down to sin, then God draws near to him, even the third time, in chastisement, in sickness, and affliction, because God wills

"To bring back his soul from the pit,
That he may be enlightened with the light of the living."

— CHAP, XXXIII. 30.

THE GRACE OF CHASTISEMENT.

Let us never be tempted to think lower things of the government of God. "No chastisement seemeth for the present to be joyous," and few of us can find joy in it. But chastisement is mercy. Punishment is grace. It is good of God and good to us to punish us when we go wrong. If we refuse to be held by the silken cords of His affection, then it is kind of Him and kind to us to reveal to us by the lightning flashes the abysses toward which our steps are tending. The author of the Letter to the Hebrews thought that "it is a fearful thing to fall into the hands of the Living God." Even if "the hands of the Living God" represent to us only catastrophe and terror, then we may be very sure that it would be a far more fearful thing to fall out of them. If we could sin with a hard heart and a determined purpose and no stroke fall upon us, if we could sow to the flesh without reaping corruption, and sow the wind of unlawful desire without reaping the whirlwind of retribution, it would be ill with us and not well, it would be cruel to us, not kind. And it is all of the mercy of our God that when we refuse to serve Him "with joyfulness, and with gladness of heart, by reason of the abundance of all things," then He causes us "to serve the enemies that the Lord shall send against thee, in hunger and in thirst, and in nakedness, and in want of all things"; and it is for our good and for our salvation that in such a case He "puts a yoke of iron" upon our neck.[2]

It is too late in the day for us to be afraid of the love of God or of the implications of our own Evangel. The theology of the middle ages contended in the mind of Dante against his large humanity. Over the gates of hell he saw written:

"All hope abandon, ye who enter here";

and a thousand times we have quoted the woeful words. We strangely forget that even in Dante's view this "city of woe" was still an expression of God's love. The same inscription reads:

"To rear me was the task of Power divine,
Supremest wisdom, and primeval love."

We know the "fear of the Lord" and we are glad to know it; knowing it we "persuade men"[3]—we do not coerce them—and we are ourselves persuaded that deep down in the lowest depths of the nethermost hell the love of God goes blazing and consuming on.

THE JUSTICE OF GOD.

In chapter xxxiv Elihu enters fully upon his reply to Job's repeated charges against the jusfice of God. He develops his argument at great length and illustrates it in many ways.[4] But the heart of it all is this: God,and injustice together are unthinkable. Elihu would not have known the meaning of our phrase, "a contradiction in terms"; yet this is what he is really saying. You may say "God" or you may say "Justice," but you cannot say "God" and "Injustice" too. They cannot be thought.

> "Far be it from God that he should do
>   wickedness,
> And from the Almighty, that he should
>   commit iniquity"
>
> — (CHAP, XXXIV. 10);

but why?

"Yea of a surety, God will not do wickedly,

Neither will the Almighty pervert justice"

— (VER. 12).

Why? Simply because God is God! The modern thinker may say, "But if I find that the system under which I live is wrong, I will not call it right; and if the course and constitution of nature are characterised by cruelty and injustice, then I will not profess that I see evidence of the rule of a wise and benevolent God." But it would not occur to Elihu or to his contemporaries to speak in this way. God is: so much is postulated. It has to be admitted before one can enter into the discussion. And Elihu is not wrong when he insists, vigorously and triumphantly, "God" and "Injustice" are absurd! He does not add argument when he insists that God's beneficence is seen in the continued existence of created things upon the earth, all sustained by His spirit and His breath:

"If he set his heart upon himself,
If he gather unto himself his spirit and his
    breath;
All flesh shall perish together,
And man shall turn again unto dust"

— (VERS. 14, 15).

But he does add emphasis. For the devout soul of

any age, learned or illiterate, feels that without God's just rule over all the earth admitted by the reason or realised by faith, the universe rolls back to chaos,

> "The pillared firmament is rottenness,
> And earth's base built on stubble."
>
> — MILTON, *COMUS*.

THE IMPOSSIBILITY OF INJUSTICE.

There is value in Elihu's rough and ready method of dealing with the problem. It may look like a swift cut at the gordian-knot just because one finds that he cannot untie it. But the method is more reasonable than it looks. If we have once said "God," and said it with all our mind and soul and strength, we have said Justice, Goodness, Mercy, Love. The suggestion which challenges these attributes is not thought: it is absurdity. When we think we are saying such things we are not saying things at all. We are using words which cancel each other out.

Fairbairn, in his most masterly discussions of the Problem of Evil, affirms that "impossibilities must exist to God as to men; possible things Omnipotence may achieve, impossible things not even Omnipotence may accomplish." And he particularises: "These inabilities or impossibilities may be said to be of three kinds: physical, intellectual, and moral. The moral inability may be stated in the familiar phrase: 'It is impossible for God to lie.' The intellectual may be represented either under the category of thought: It is impossible for God to conceive the false as if it were true; or under the category of knowledge: It is impossible for God to know things that are not as if they were real things. The physical impossibility may be expressed in various forms: It is not open even to God to make a part equal to the whole; to make the same thing both be and not be; to make a circle at once a circle and a square, or to make a square out of two straight lines."[5]

And the point, of course, is that God cannot make a human being who should *start* as if he had a long experience behind him or an acquired character within. So that the experiences of life, conflict, pain, temptation are unavoidable if there is to be on earth such a being as man. The conclusion is indisputable, but the explanations about things which are impossible to Almightiness are superfluous. It is simpler to say that these "impossibilities" represent only our own incapacity for thinking or the inherent incapacity of words for conveying thought By a square we mean the space that is enclosed by four straight lines, and when we say that two cannot enclose a square we are merely playing tricks with words. The limitation is not in the power of God but in our ability to see that we are not seeing at all! Nine-tenths of the common difficulties connected with the existence of evil slip into the background when we remember the first law of thought, that "a thing cannot both be and not be at the same time." God is: that is Elihu's postulate—and ours. In Him a deflection from Justice, Goodness, Mercy, Love is unthinkable. It contradicts the primary law of thought.

LOVE AS JUSTICE.

It is significant that Elihu, who gives fresh emphasis and point to the contention of the three friends as to God's unfailing justice, is the one who brings into prominence the mercifulness of God's approach to the man in danger of yielding to sin, the approach in dreams, in visions and their interpretation, and in affliction. Is it going too far, is it ascribing to Elihu modern conceptions of which he was incapable, if we find in the whole of the second part of chapter xxxiii an undefined conviction that God's justice demands this mercifulness? Did Elihu see that it would not be just of God to leave a man alone, unwarned, unsought, unredeemed? It is amongst the deepest notes of the Gospel: in some unrealised way was Elihu feeling after the truth of it? "If we confess our sins, he is faithful and righteous to forgive us our sins."[6] *Righteous*! It is just of Him to do it, and it would not be just not to do it! He owes it to Himself, to the everlasting rectitude of His holy name! "Never in all your preaching admit that the Atonement is demanded by the justice of God," a theological teacher now dead used to say to his students; "insist that the Atonement grows out of God's love."[7] Yet what if God's love and His justice are not two but one? If His justice is the same thing as His love, if He loves because it is *just* that He should? When we warn men and women to beware of God's justice and close with the offers of His love, how we misconceive and misrepresent Him! Because He is just we can trust His love, for ever and for ever we can trust the love of a God who is just.

> "Thank God that God shall judge my soul,
>   not man!
> I marvel when they say,
> 'Think of that awful Day —
> No pitying fellow-sinner's eyes shall scan
> With tolerance thy soul,
> But His who knows the whole,
> The God whom all men own is wholly just.'
> Hold thou that last word dear,
> And live untouched by fear.
> He knows with what strange fires He mixed
>   this dust.
> The heritage of race,
> The circumstance and place
> Which make us what we are—were from His
>   hand,
> That left us, faint of voice,
> Small margin for a choice.
> He gave, I took: shall I not fearless stand?
> Hereditary bent

> That hedges in intent
> He knows, be sure, the God who shaped thy
>   brain.
> He loves the souls He made;
> He knows His own hand laid
> On each the mark of some ancestral stain.
> Not souls severely white,
> But groping for more light,
> Are what Eternal Justice here demands.
> Fear not; He made thee dust.
> Cling to that sweet word—'Just'
> All's well with thee if thou art in just hands."
>
> — ANNA REEVE ALDRICH.

---

1. For the reasons which lead to this unqualified conclusion the reader is referred to the larger commentaries. A lengthy critical discussion would be outside the purpose of the Short Course Series. W. T. Davison's article on "Job" in Hastings' *Dictionary of the Bible* should by all means be consulted.
2. Deuteronomy xxviii. 47-8.
3. 2 Corinthians v. 11.
4. The preacher will do well to construct his own analysis of the Elihu speeches contained in chaps. xxxii.-xxxvii., and he cannot do better than take Davidson for guide.
5. Fairbairn, *The Philosophy of the Christian Religion*.
6. 1 John i. 9.
7. The late Thomas Goadby, Principal of the Midland Baptist College.

CHAPTER 8
THE SPEECHES OF JEHOVAH

"Gird up now thy loins like a man," is the peremptory call of Jehovah when He "answers Job out of the whirlwind." It is an echo of the demand which the author must have made upon himself as he approached the climax of his splendid work. He sets his nerves at a strain for the tremendous task which lay before him in fitting speeches to the character of Jehovah. Upon it he brought all his mighty powers to bear. He gave free wing to his imagination while calling to his aid all the knowledge of all his world. The result is worthy, of his ambitions, his consecration, and his toil. In this noble book there is nothing nobler, in this work of genius there is nothing more sublime, than the speeches of Jehovah.

Quotation is difficult because of the wealth of the whole. Where all is pure gold one hesitates which nugget to pick up. But the music of some of the lines will never pass out of human speech. Phrases from this part of *Job* are in our hymns, our prayers, our sermons, and they will be treasured in the liturgy of the Church of God for ever. The day will never dawn in which we cease to ascribe praises to the Almighty and Everlasting God who "laid the foundations of the earth" and the corner-stone thereof—

> "When the morning stars sang together,
> And all the sons of God shouted for joy";

who alone is able to

> "Bind the cluster of the Pleiades
> Or loose the bands of Orion";

and say to the advancing sea,

> "Hitherto shalt thou come, but no further;
> And here shall thy proud wares be stayed."

Truly, the author of this divine drama has "girded up his loins like a man," and given to the world pictures and phrases which the world will never let die!

THE "ANSWER" OF JEHOVAH.

"Then Jehovah answered Job out of the whirlwind, and said" —. What did He say? "Moreover, Jehovah answered Job, and said"—Twice the formula appears; but what did He say?

Nothing, absolutely nothing, nothing that touches the point of Job's complainings, nothing that meets his demands, nothing that is *ad rem*. He appears, as Job had wished Him to appear, as the Creator and Ruler of the universe, clothed upon with its glories, its terrors, and its mysteries. He comes to answer Job's reverently irreverent challenges and silence objections which the heart of the man had flung out against the course and constitution of His world. And He says—nothing! He asserts what has not been denied and proves what nobody has called in question. And Job is satisfied! For Job answered Jehovah and said:

> "Therefore have I uttered that which I understood not,
> Things too wonderful for me which I knew not...
> Wherefore I repudiate my words[1]
> And repent in dust and ashes."
>
> —JOB XLII. 6.

Herein lies no mystery. The genius of our author

has not betrayed him. His method is true to the facts of human experience. The revelation of God is made to the heart, not to the brain: His spirit operates within the sphere of the emotions, and only afterwards and by way of reflex action in the region of the intellect. With the heart man believeth unto righteousness.

Illustrations of the working of this law in contemporary life and literature are innumerable. It holds good even of those processes by which some storm-tossed soul finds peace when one would hesitate to ascribe the result to the leadings of God's spirit! Hundreds of men—the keenest intellects of the nineteenth century—tried in one way or another to analyse John Henry Newman's *Apologia pro vita sua*. None succeeds in doing it. To this day nobody can say why Newman left the Anglican Church for the Roman—unless, of course, one is ready to give an explanation which Newman would have scorned. One follows with the keenest delight, with intellectual joy and spiritual zest, the carefully written account of his thoughts and feelings through many years. But when the crucial hour dawns and one supposes that he is now to see "the moving why" Newman made the change and how the change satisfied his soul, one is led up to a blank wall and left staring at it. For all the explanation given the *Apologia* might as well have remained unwritten. It would have served to say: "Then I decided to enter the Roman Communion." If Newman was an inscrutable enigma to Charles Kingsley before the *Apologia* saw the light of day, he must have been something more puzzling still after it appeared ! And one of the really memorable things in the fruitful annals of the Oxford Movement and its consequences is the fact that Gladstone, after his close and intimate friendship with Manning, should at last shake his head and say in bewilderment: "Manning was not straight!" "Straight" we may gladly concede such conduct essentially is; *clear* it certainly is not

A more helpful illustration is found nearer to hand. Some years ago an English journalist, possessed of a taking, slap-dash newspaper style, and having a large following amongst earnest, true-hearted, but uneducated young men and women, galvanised into a show of life the old Bradlaugh-Ingersoll materialism which had been practically lost sight of on both sides of the Atlantic before the death of those two men. There was one good result. A host of Christian controversialists were quickly in the field, and these assaults upon faith were repelled with a vigour and effectiveness which flung into bold relief the feebleness and folly of the atheistic propaganda. Amongst the replies was a volume entitled *Religious Doubts of the Democracy*. The writers, fifteen in number, included Mr. Chesterton, Mr. George W. E. Russell, and Dr. Fry. Three of the writers gave an account of their own doubts and conquest of doubt. They told how they had lost faith and how they fought their way back to it. Two were working men, one a trained thinker, the headmaster of a public school. Their stories are admirably told—only, one is little wiser when he has read them 1 The precise thing which for each one laid doubt low and brought back the soul to God is still to seek. Each one is satisfied, as Job is satisfied, not because God has supplied the ground of intellectual assent to dogma, but because He has revealed Himself to the waiting heart. He has "answered" out of the whirlwind.

THE VALUE OF CHRISTIAN EVIDENCES.

So understood, and so interpreted, this section of *Job* raises for us the question of the value of that form of apologetic known as "Christian evidences."

Every apologetic is relative, relative to the individual to whom it is addressed, to his temperament, his training, the stage of development he has reached, and the mood in which it finds him. When the preacher is asked for "evidences of Christianity," it would be a perfectly proper thing for him to ask, "What sort of evidence do you want?" For it is as important to know the sort of evidence the inquirer *wants* as to know the sort he needs. Yet in the long run it will be found that the value of "evidences" is slight. They rarely produce fruits of holiness. Superior to the reasonings and conclusions of all logic are the deliverances of our human affection. We love, but we can with difficulty say why we love. To this day the lover finds no newer answer to the familiar question, "Why do you love me?" than the time-honoured formula, "Because you are you!" And the one way which God has provided for the discovery of Himself is that of a powerful emotional yearning toward goodness. If a man *willeth* to do His will, he shall know of the teaching.[2]

Nevertheless, good work may be done by the Christian apologist who can show the objector that his objections are not final. The doubter may be made to feel that his objections carry him too far; that they may be urged with equal strength against the things of which he is most deeply persuaded; and that if he will follow where they lead he may end in denying everything. This is the Butler method in the famous *Analogy*. Hugh Price Hughes was in the habit of saying that the *Analogy* had never "saved a soul" since it was written. In his sense of the phrase, it was not intended to "save a soul." It said to men of a certain day who professed a certain half-religious theory of the universe, "You decline to accept Christianity because of specific objections; yet those objections can be urged with precisely the same force against the philosophy you hold and defend. This is not reasonable." The principle is sound, and the application of it is dangerous only because the person who has taken refuge in a half-faith may be driven to say, "True! and I will abandon the remnant of faith to which I was clinging!" Gladstone, whose admiration for Bishop Butler knew no bounds, used the method in homely fashion to far better purpose than his great teacher did. For he insisted that such objections as were urged against Christianity could be urged against things which no human being can give up—and live! His argument is unanswerable: —

> "For Doubt I have a sincere respect, but Doubt and Scepticism are different things. I contend that the sceptic is of all men on earth the most inconsistent and irrational. He uses a plea against religion which he never uses against anything he wants to do or any idea he wants to embrace—viz., the want of demonstrative evidence. Every day and all day long he is acting on evidence not demonstrative: he eats the dish he likes without certainty that it is not poisoned; he rides the horse he likes without certainty that the animal will not break his neck; he sends out of the house a servant he suspects without demonstration of guilt; he marries the woman he likes with no absolute knowledge that she loves him; he embraces the political opinion that he likes, perhaps without any study at all, certainly without demonstrative evidence of its truth. But when he comes to religion he is seized with a great intellectual scrupulosity, and demands as a pre-condition of homage to God what every-

where else he dispenses with, and then ends with thinking himself more rational than other people."³

THE SOUL SUBDUED BY VASTNESS.

So Job is silenced before he is satisfied. And he is silenced by a vision of the vastness of the universe. Before his eyes the limitless panorama of nature is unrolled, and as his gaze reaches from wonder to wonder and from glory to glory his confidence in his own right or power to "contend" with the Most High weakens within him. Jehovah "answers" him out of the whirlwind, answers with questions, with demands, with merciless, dominating inquiries which strip him of the last vestige of "superiority" in which he had clothed himself as with a garment, and leave him silent and ashamed:

> "Hast *thou* commanded the morning since
>   thy days began,
> And caused the dayspring to know its place?
>   • • • • • •
> Hast thou entered into the springs of the sea?
> Or hast thou walked in the recesses of the
>   deep?
> Have the gates of death been revealed unto
>   thee?
>   • • • • • •
> Where is the way to the dwelling of light?

And as for darkness, where is the place
    thereof?
• • • • • •
Doubtless thou knowest, for thou wast then
    born,
And the number of thy days is great!"

The irony is terrible. Is it deserved? At least, it does its work. Job is overwhelmed by the universe. These things belong only unto God:

"I know that thou canst do all things,
And that no purpose of thine can be re-
    strained."

He repeats Jehovah's question,

"Who is this that hideth counsel without
    knowledge?"

And the guilty one stands self-confessed: it is himself!

An English poet translates the wonder and the awe of Job into the terms of modern science. Astronomy has made more vast the vastness which overwhelmed and silenced Job. To the devout soul it has made "doubt" still more untenable.

"And thro' all the clear spaces above— oh
    wonder! oh glory of Light! —

Came forth myriads on myriads of worlds,
    the shining host of the night, —

The vast forces and fires that know the same
    sun and centre as we;
The faint planets which roll in vast orbits
    round suns we shall never see;

The rays which had sped from the first, with
    the awful swiftness of light,
To reach only then, it might be, the confines
    of mortal sight:

Oh, wonder of Cosmical Order! oh, Maker
    and Ruler of all,
Before whose Infinite greatness in silence we
    worship and fall!

Could I doubt that the Will which keeps this
    great Universe steadfast and sure
Might be less than His creatures thought, full
    of goodness, pitiful, pure?

Could I dream that the Power which keeps
    those great suns circling round,
Took no thought for the humblest life which
    flutters and falls to the ground?"

And the conclusion is the last word of wisdom as it is the first of religion,

> "Oh, Faith! thou art higher than all."
>
> — LEWIS MORRIS, *EVENSONG.*

THE EPILOGUE.

The epilogue, it has already been pointed out, "adds nothing to the grandeur of the poem." It adds nothing to our understanding of life's mysteries and nothing to the faith that soars above them. It is a part of the "machinery" of the drama. For the purpose of his drama, by way of bringing his characters upon the stage, our author exposed Job to calamities and sorrows. The purpose accomplished, the case tried and verdict rendered, poetic justice demands that Job should be restored to his former estate of prosperity and recompensed for his losses. It is done with oriental completeness and lavishness. Job lives a hundred and forty years longer, lives in the smiles of fortune, and at last, full of years and honour, comes to his grave, as Eliphaz hoped he might,

> "Like m a shock of grain cometh in in its
>   season."

But it would have been better for us if *Job* had never been born of the brain of one of earth's noblest thinkers than for us to think that this, in the end, is to be the reward of righteousness. Let us believe this and act upon our belief and then the Satan's question may justly be addressed to us: Do we serve God for nought? Bread was never the reward of virtue. Houses and land, wealth in mounded heaps, and the delights of the children of men are not the recompense of faith and hope and love. The great man of letters whose study of *Job* remains, when all is said and done, the most searching and suggestive and satisfying in the literature of two continents, asks us to fling scorn upon so base and debasing a view of man's relations with the Infinite. And as these expositions opened with his characterisation of the divine drama, they may well close with his characterisation of religion:—

"If Christianity had never borne itself more loftily than this, do we suppose that those fierce Norsemen who had learnt, in the fiery war-songs of the Edda, of what stuff the hearts of heroes are composed, would have fashioned their sword-hilts into crosses and themselves into a crusading chivalry? Let us not dishonour our great fathers with the dream of it. The Christians, like the Stoics and the Epicureans, would have lived their little day among the ignoble sects of an effete civilisation, and would have passed off and been heard of no more. It was in another spirit that those first preachers of righteousness went out upon their warfare with evil. They preached, not enlightened prudence, but purity, justice, goodness; holding out no promises in this world except of suffering as their great Master had suffered, and rejoicing that they were counted worthy to suffer for His sake. And that crown of glory which they did believe to await them in a life beyond the grave, was no enjoyment of what they had surrendered in life, was not enjoyment at all in any sense which human thought or language can attach to the words, . . . it was to be with Christ—to lose themselves in Him."[4]

These words are true and righteous altogether. In the truth of them our souls abide. From the reading of this heroic poem we shall rise in heroic mood if it has bred in us the confidence that the "reward" of Christianity is—Christ.

---

1. "repudiate" or "retract" my words, not "abhor myself."
2. John vii. 17.
3. *Gladstone's Letters on Church and Religion* (edited by D. C. Lathbury), vol. ii. pp. 77-78.
4. Froude, *Short Studies on Great Subjects: The Book of Job*.

APPENDIX

SOME ADDITIONAL READING

In the foregoing pages and footnotes the author has cited some of the best and most easily accessible literature on the Book of Job. No one who is designing a course of lectures on this "greatest poem of ancient or modern times" could do better than turn to the works so justly recommended:—J. A. Froude's *Short Studies on Great Subjects* (1867); A. B. Davidson's *The Book of Job*, in the "Cambridge Bible for Schools"(1884), or his article "Job" in the *Ency. Brit*, eleventh edition; W. T. Davison's *The Wisdom Literature* (1894), or his article "Job" in Hastings' *Dictionary of the Bible.* These all supply expository material of the highest practical value, and may well be consulted by the teacher or preacher in the framing of his discourse.

To these may be added three other works of the same outstanding character, (1) A. M. Fairbairn's *The City of God*, pp. 143-189 (1886)—a fine appreciation of the "nameless man," who so lived and wrestled that "the thoughts that possessed him, the faith that consoled him, and the hopes that transmuted and glorified his sorrows, are set here as to everlasting music." (2) T. K. Cheyne's admirable article on "Job" in the *Ency. Biblica*—a study which, with all its emendations and grammatical details (warning Paseks, and the rest) is yet pre-eminently lucid and suggestive, and never fails to do justice to that "inextinguishable heart-religion" which is surely one of the leading features of this great psychological drama. (3) As a perfect mine of expository material, however, we must make special mention of the latest study in this age-long problem—James Strahan's supremely able and spiritually alive volume, *The Book of Job* (1913. For the purposes of a wise and practical exposition, based upon a sound and illuminating exegesis, we hail this contribution to Old Testament literature as one of the best books of its kind. Open it where one may, one instinctively feels that he is under the guidance of a master. Is it the description of the *writer of the poem* as contained in the finely conceived *Introduction*? "He resembles the prophets of his race in his high and imperious standard of right, his flaming hatred of wrong. His expanding opinions only intensify his moral sense. His strenuous thinking is no less remarkable than his consummate literary art" Or is it the sigh of conscious rectitude, longing to come near to God, that the maligned one may be delivered *from his judge* (xxiii. 3, 7)? We are at once pointed to the much better rendering of the LXX:—"so should I forever *recover my right*." "Job asks for a trial, not in order that he may be delivered from his Judge, but that he may hear his Judge vindicate his innocence and give him back his good name as an everlasting possession." Once more, is it the thought of death extinguishing the faint gleam of an after-life, as depicted in xiv. 14, and forcing the patriarch to exclaim —

> "Thou prevailed for ever against him, and *he passeth*;
> Thou changest his countenance, and sendest him away"?

He passeth! The attention of the reader is directed at once to the significance of this figure, and he is asked to see in it the inspiring teaching of Revelation, no less than the sombre language of nature. "But if Revelation consents to retain the word 'passeth,'"4 she does so only on the condition that she shall be allowed to give it an entirely new content; for her teaching is that *'we have passed* out of death into life' (1 John iii. 14), so that at the last 'there is no death, what seems so is transition.' The 'Passing of Arthur' is not a descent, dreaded by the ancients, into an underworld of darkness, but a going to meet the dawn." Or, finally, if we turn to the great crucial passage in chapter xix., and read —

"Oh that my words were now written!
Oh that they were inscribed in a book!"

Could anything be more suggestive than the comment—"how splendidly his idea has been realised! His singular fancy of a testimony *in the rocks* could not be gratified, but he has his *apologia*—his *monumentum ære perennius*—in a *book* which is the masterpiece of Hebrew poetic genius."

All this is biblical exegesis at his best; and no one should attempt the exposition of the Book of Job without consulting the wealth of homiletical hint and sound Bible teaching contained in this painstaking and admirable volume.

J.A.

Copyright © 2024 by Alicia EDITIONS
Credits: www.canva.com; Alicia EDITIONS, illustration by John Gilbert, painter (21 July 1817 – 5 October 1897), The book of JOB; 1857.
PAPERBACK : 9782384552559
E-BOOK: 9782384552566
HARDCOVER: 9782384552573
All rights reserved.
No part of this book may be reproduced in any form or by any electronic or mechanical means, including information storage and retrieval systems, without written permission from the author, except for the use of brief quotations in a book review.

www.ingramcontent.com/pod-product-compliance
Lightning Source LLC
LaVergne TN
LVHW032013070526
838202LV00059B/6425